Le

Lent

Martyn Halsall

wild goose publications

www.ionabooks.com

First published 2025 by
Wild Goose Publications
Suite 9, Fairfield, 1048 Govan Road, Glasgow G51 4XS, Scotland
A division of Iona Community Trading CIC
Limited Company Reg. No. SC156678
www.ionabooks.com

ISBN 978-1-80432-374-8

Cover image © Fiona Hislop, from her painting 'Windblown Sand'
www.etsy.com/uk/shop/fIONAcolours

Overseas distribution
Australia: Willow Connection Pty Ltd, 1/13 Kell Mather Drive,
Lennox Head NSW 2478
New Zealand: Pleroma, Higginson Street, Otane 4170, Central Hawkes Bay

Printed in the UK by Page Bros (Norwich) Ltd

MIX
Paper | Supporting responsible forestry
FSC® C023114
FSC www.fsc.org

Contents

To Isobel,
who made it possible

Introduction

Lent is always with us. While officially confined to forty days of developing Spring in the Christian calendar its essential themes of wilderness, pilgrimage, exile and alienation are demanding, and persistent. They shadow us, and raise issues of who we are becoming; where we are going. These poems aim to reflect on this, and are offered as potential passports and signposts through challenging times.

Poetry is never straightforward, otherwise it would be prose. It does not travel in straight lines but deviates, pauses, awarding time to the intriguing, and the peripheral. It is open to being sidetracked, detained, diverted. In that sense it is the natural language of official Lent, and its demands for stillness, silence and reappraisal.

Poetry is also concerned with alternatives. It does not assert, but asks rather: 'What if?', and answers: 'Yes, but…'. It remains unconvinced by any single meaning. So with these poems, where 'Lent' is both a Christian season, but also a notification of process; an acknowledgement that human life is both gift and borrowing, something that for a relatively short time within history's pilgrimage we are 'lent'.

The Irish writer Michael Longley said that if he knew where poems came from he would go there. One such destination is memory, whether from years ago or recent experience, impelling that reaching for a biro and a scrap of paper; that mystery of why some things – people, places, objects, events among them – stay with us and demand representation and analysis, that interrogated record from which poetry is formed.

This collection therefore opens with some memories of lent

life. It begins at first light when, as a young journalist in Oxford, I would pedal along the towpath to note the Radio Oxford headlines, and scan and clip the national newspapers for any reference to the life of the university city we were recording. But what is 'news'? Is it the official agendas of state and church, the recorded minutes and strategies of institutions, or the side glances, and the pausing spaces; what stays with us, the lent that is retained after the official record has been dictated?

Our own histories prosecute that argument; beyond the official paperwork; what we remember; how that might be filtered, and even reimagined. So the opening section, 'Memoir', also includes anecdotal history that my parents recounted from their lent lives, memories of days when my life changed, or preparations as varied as a first visit to fell country where Lancashire, Yorkshire and Cumbria intermingle, or borrowing time from the long history of an abbey. 'Memoir' also reintroduces moments of bereavement. Shadow, suicide and storm condition memory for many. They are part of the poetic quest of alternative possibilities: those 'What ifs', those other stories that might have been written, the elevation of alternatives.

'Lent', the second section, uses the Christian season as springboard; poetry's potential for honouring the side glances. Poems wander, in different directions and through varying experiences, as they aim to analyse in the quiet that follows movement and exploration. This is the stillness of older people turning the pages of a photograph album where images rekindle memories. Poems here edge towards the historic Easter while also containing the contemporary; the overshadowing of a friend's death, for example, alongside the continuing suffering of the peoples of Palestine and Israel. Beyond and around is the ever-present optimism of Christ's resurrection.

Within the Christian community, and arguably more widely, there is also a growing realisation of the need to lament, to cast aside the temptations of judgementalism, and adopt the intercessory heart. This conditions the final section of these poems. Guides emerge from both inside and beyond formal church structures; Rembrandt with his confessional self-interrogation, or the poet-priest RS Thomas, bilingual in the shadow-language within faith, and its questioning. Death becomes more familiar as we grow older, taking friends, or people we knew only by literary association, into whatever follows our borrowed times.

With each exercise of revising and gathering poems towards a collection there has to come a moment of recognition that a final poem has arrived. That may be an event, or an overhearing. News of the death of the Scottish writer John Burnside suggested such a moment. He was often outside, the dark coat of a lingering Catholic heritage mantling his shoulders. His work is deeply involved in such contemporary awareness as the flickering shadow-play of a spiritual concern for planetary survival. Much of his poetry seems to summon the dusk where we are called to lament; the other end of the day from where we set out to see what 'the news' might offer.

Lent continues, not least in the anguish of broken people and their communities, and a world at war with its own future. We are poised, at this end of Lent, in the lent light of any Easter Saturday that awaits a resurrection. It is into this Lenten tension that these poems are offered.

Ovington, Northumberland
Feast of the Transfiguration 2024

Memoir

Electric Blue

First light: bike tyres sizzled as the dynamo
clicked to the rim, and powered up a fitful beam;
wheels within wheels, down side roads to the towpath.

Thin dawn seeped back, outlining silhouettes;
charcoal of wintering trees, a wash of orange
tinting the water to a watercolour

as tarmac's hum changed down for wash of gravel,
mudguards lined red and brown with speckled clay,
then three-speed in top gear along the level

fast-pedalling through gathering detail for the early shift
to list the radio headlines, clip the papers;
the water boatmen crews skimming meniscus.

A blue flash flared as if rehearsing lightning,
setting another agenda for that morning.
Not that a small bird spearing air would counter

the news list with its accidents and inquests.
Yet it stayed vivid; still comes to life again
whenever the world turns natural, and electric.

The Greatcoat

A quiet Saturday on an evening paper;
sort of slack water a trainee might be sent
to try and find a story among some jumble,
and come back with a line about a march-past;

a single file, the shade of threatening weather,
of RAF surplus greatcoats chiming hangers,
each carpet thickness cloth with wingspan epaulettes,
flare path of buttons, leading edge square pockets

area of map case, or an unsent letter.
And on another stall that novel *The Greatcoat*
raising a question: Do we then become
another, in another person's greatcoat?

Deep in the book a spirit tapped a window,
Lancaster captain morsing glass for entrance.
The coat's long gone: recalling it would wear
that uniform as ghost; a bomber's flightpath.

History

A bomber's moon; the gradual gnaw of engines
threading through shafts of searchlights, following flares,
aiming for my father's billet, my mother's factory
where other bombers were built, parachutes packaged.

Their stories grew into history; like my father
going on leave across a well-known city,
and losing his way in streets no longer standing,
stumbling in blackout over hose intestines;

or like my mother who felt foundations tremble
during raids on armaments factories miles away;
who saw bus passengers with bagged-up bundles,
all they could salvage after the house came down.

Danger is hearing stories simply as history,
and never deciphering parables. Perhaps
holding a bowl in an anxious queue for rations,
or turned away from the trauma of a bloodied ward,

we might know for ourselves an immediate sorrow.
For now, we follow the present while it's light,
taking the immediate as a frame of reference;
snowdrops below stripped blackthorn, sprouts of hawthorn.

Moon

Perhaps it was something one of my parents said,
or one of the very first things that I remember
of turning a circular tin lid over and over.

Writing on one side, labelling a sort of polish,
and slightly scarred where a snagged catch prised it open,
yellow and black, perhaps, as lunar and crater.

Other side silver as a flat, full moon,
an alternative view I'd find with each revolution,
turning it back to eclipse, over and over.

Perhaps it defined the future, hanging about
in a cleared sky summoning frost through a wintering orchard.
A glance from a track would find it stilled, and waiting
as though whoever had coined it had left it haunted.

Spade

History lies heavy; take my father's spade,
cross-handle sheened from days when he could use it
to turn new ground, dig garden from the former marsh,
blade given a turn where once it rang a boulder.

Alliance of ash and steel where shaft was forged
to sheathe the head with welded bolt, or rivet
holding it fast for seventy, eighty years,
becoming redundant, left to lighter followers.

My father was never much of a digging man
despite his father, a Corporation gardener,
winning the village prize for the bloom of his beds.
I remember his tools, rusting in a splintering shed.

Perhaps that spade was his pride, a handing-down,
already clarted with years at his wartime death,
not bomb or bullet, just a passing away
as a gardener might come to his trees for evening quiet.

Everything new for my parents; their post-war house,
fuchsia and poppies, a pair of apple saplings
made aerials by sea breezes, as listening in;
their gratitude for peace they defined as Eden.

That spade came with us for years, from house to house,
strung up in sheds, crosspiece across two nails,
its blade a bass note if a door banged shut.
Now I try to remember what became of it.

Class

All afternoon classes were being sorted
for O level year; a call to the headmaster's study
brought promotion into Trans Modern, gave the chance
to take both History and English Literature.

Next afternoon a recall to the headmaster's study
for a sort of apology; somebody had to drop out
from the oversubscribed Upper Five Trans Modern,
to choose between History and English Literature.

Most afternoons seemed all the same, a fading
of light as words were copied across inked pages.
Some offered ways forward, or seemed to suggest directions
down narrow ways to high places. Some afternoons

the lesson was simply leaving the world as it was.
On others you learned about privilege, and class.

Breaking News

Each day began with a bag of folded headlines
across a shoulder, listing to take the weight
as I set out, balancing the angled bike.

Still night those winter mornings, ribs of ice
rigid as steel rails, angled banks of snow
laid out like shrouds along familiar roads.

Forest and Chambres, all the length of Lethbridge;
time between gate and letterbox to scan
front pages with their histories, prophecies:

Great Freeze Set to Continue; Famous Poet
Found Dead in London Flat. I was the first
to break the news, before the wireless spoke.

Perhaps, after the crossword, one reader might
have opened her poems again, in retrospect,
having learned how she had left the children's breakfast
of bread and milk before turning on the gas?

Light seeped through seaside streets as I got back,
leaving the newsprint-black, draped empty bag
below the shelves of boiled sweets, and fags.

School in an hour, but that first lesson learned
of gathering stories, setting history out,
reading and writing; becoming part of it.

Carvers' Marks

Eternity's been here since the twelfth century
when masons first split local stones to draft
cathedral's bone and form each spring and summer,

retreating into shelter when weather lapsed
to carve the next instalment of column, moulding,
to find in strata and grain one laughing morning

archdeacon cloned to gargoyle with bared arse,
a Green Man spying through oak; a basking dragon.

Few left their names, though some a clue in runes.
Rather their signatures were carvers' marks
that nicked medieval centuries in their wanderings.

Here, at year's ending, where the map turns North,
we take blessed evidence of ordered stone,
still catching fire at the far end of sunlight.

Interior Landscape

The woman was turned to stone; robes' pleats and folds
made ridges and valleys of interior landscape.
She has no name. Her face is now worn raw
as a river boulder, or victim of pox outbreak.

She lies still in the barely shifting light
as sketched in charcoal; vacancy, possibly sorrow
shading her like the boundary of a wood
winter has moved to, seeking sanctuary.

Or like an estuary; chiselled curves suggest
channels of swirl, and oiled light dredged by ebb.
Perhaps in her dream she hears a gull cry out.
An otter is curled in rumpled cloth at her feet.

Whoever worked this stone has read its ground
as pattern and form, brought to that triangular
interlock of carving a runrig or pilgrims' track,
a weave of drapery like roots' overlap.

Except that the space where her long rest is laid
is squared off. Her gaze is fixed, as if to sky
framed through stone's arching tracery of boughs,
and infills' rippled shadow of storm warning.

Her history seems always chilled. She might have thought
future would not be like this, rather grown
warm, and people recognised in retranslation
of body and blood; nourishing, like bread and wine.

Those who pass by at slow-motion, death march pace
read the brief caption labelling her, and a companion:
Two unknown women, fourteenth century, catch
something of psalms in woods, like an overhearing.

Free

The last seven rows, marked *Free*, right at the back,
were out of sight of priest and people, hidden
by pillars as wide and tall as governing classes.

Those pointed there would only see the backs
of betters paying pew rents for their access,
would have to wait till land, and wealth, filed out.

They were kept a decent distance from the altar,
screened behind carving, stone, could steam if rain
detained them behind decanting carriages,

would catch downcasting glances from strict ushers
if they voiced fervour in a hymn or creed.
Meekness demanded that they knew their places

and kept thoughts to themselves about a teacher
whose blessings of the poor were best glossed over,
whose father, like their own, was artisan,
and would have known what wood a cross was made from.

Texts

Eight hundred post-it notes add to the texts
the abbey has said and sung for fourteen centuries.
These messages are the colour of Ukraine's flags,
deep blue of summer skies, yellow as barley.

So many that some go skittering to the floor
as organ begins its practice, invading silence.
Many read simply *Peace*, the hardest prayer,
many are layered like roof tiles, curled at edges.

Some children left self-portraits, gave their names,
left questions: *are you oakay god and Jesase?*
I love Ukraine: Nikita from Kyiv.
Another adds: *help people hoo are indujued.*

Encouragement: *Stay strong, and we'll bring him down.*
Judgement: *Kill Putin – resist Russian oppression.*
Kickass, above the injunction *Peace for all.*
A rifle is sketched above a CND sign.

Poetry takes root around a flower drawing:
Like a sunflower, Ukraine, stand tall and strong.
Names make a postscript: *Daisy, London, Jesus.*
Stingrays support Ukraine! Postscript Cyrillic.

Beyond the noticeboard white textile poppies
mediate history with these slips of paper,
remembering *Heroes of the Battlefield*,
first global conflict of the previous century.

While over the road new comradeship of exile
has drawn Ukrainian strangers into friendship.
The library lends warmth and space to air their language
among the wealth of words in fact, and fiction.

Single

Years ago, rattling west across Czechoslovakia,
a young woman with a duffel bag, hearing English,
mimed at the dark floor space in our compartment,
changed into Party overalls; disappeared.

Eastern Europe passed. Our hosts had laughed
at our souvenir Leninist posters. Border guards
flipped our passport pages, stamped
exit visas, never checked the seating.

Passage from east to west was also hiding,
ducked out of sight in a cutting. We imagined
miles of pines, then cleared ground scanned by watchtowers,
though ash-black crows were the only others crossing.

West, and the woman left with a grateful bow.
Year later, and instead of buying glassware
or ordering dumplings in a cellar restaurant,
we might have watched those grinding Russian tanks

through half-drawn curtains, had we stayed in Prague.
Perhaps the woman who crossed the border with us
kept the return stub of her railway ticket
as bookmark in the phrase book she adopted.

The Japanese Department

Before they closed The Japanese Department
a visitor could stay on after questions
about haiku or tea ceremony, wait to catch

some context in that courtyard of raked gravel,
stones swirled to grammar, declension in the fountain;
that paradox of distance being closeness.

Flying to Osaka as the cherry blossom
frothed in the same pink as a park in England,
brought interchange of memories and image:

a china teapot with a bamboo handle,
world's largest wooden Buddha carved at Nara,
cans of hot tea a slot machine delivered,

and from the rural past a recreation,
traditional farm room on the seventieth floor
with sleeping mat rolled out, and wooden bolster.

Something was poised, like droplets in that fountain,
a scribble of time like some calligraphy,
on visiting cards of hotel pillow haiku;
that borrowed space, like memories, flying with us.

Haiku

Quakers bought this ground,
ten shillings in old coinage;
sowed a peace garden.

To build a world, take
ground, turning it to fellscape;
limestone, beech; curlew.

Fluent in hedgerows
you read woodbine, dog rose, thyme;
add stonecrop, stitchwort.

Peacock butterflies
covered rogue buddleia as
we prepared to leave.

Remember marshes;
wild geese strung across childhood:
forecast of parting.

Like left hand reaching
for sky, to close a skylight,
summer slips away.

No longer curlew
on the high moors, but autumn
winds bring ghost echoes.

Those mourning spaces;
ruined walls, children's voices:
rain on the machair.

Meeting Place

In theory rounding numbers to make a foursome.
New roads, then pulling off beside a barn,
suddenly there. Mixed bag of cottages,
a hamlet given its presence by the fells.

Low beams, and sherry; sitting-room making welcome.
Even indoors a sense of going further.
Later, a twist of lanes up to the moor.

Meeting place of three counties; underground
veined limestone caves and caverns. The ancient farm
now cavers' barn, headquarters to all directions.

Me new to curlew space; you home from home
as setting the record straight, as an unfolding
map on your life. Fell song and revelation.
That wild bird on the wind; the future, opening.

Whaup

(for Isobel)

1.

Embodied; a tumble of beck gravel worn by water,
mottled to plumage, bill echoing hand scythe curve
of a new moon's blade. Fluid call of beach, or strand:

in flight a glide to spread a wake of music:
closer, from camouflaged hide, a plod and stab,
that wader at low tide, to spear the ebb.

They defy invisibility, at half a mile
their call the only witness. Three rivers bring
fells' fresh to tidal salt of winter quarters.

Their cry's drawn landward as a calling-card;
dusk fades with echo, echo, echo; echo.

2.

That first time when your kindness took us home –
an established couple, me to make the four –
you shared your North, cottage and fellscaped moor,

far-reaching sky, the season's beckoning
as if a pilgrimage was setting out.

You were our guide, knowing those lanes to wildness,
that lonely farm dropped down below the wind,
and curlew flung to Spring over horizons

seeding the closing moment with lament,
implanting something strange; holding the note.

Wedding Day

Strange when you think of wedding days. You start
with all that finery, unaccustomed suit,
that dress unseen till now, worn just for hours,
that pocket checked, re-checked, for ring and speech.

Centre of pace, yet wanting it to pause,
to savour details, listen carefully
to all the words, prepared, what's left unsaid;
revaluing of small-change conversations.

Waving away, and suddenly just the two.
Strange roads that bring a transient destination,
new registration, with united names;

and gradually the ebbing light declines
intrusion, and as finery's set aside
there comes another knowing, before the dark.

Magnolia Shadows

For all we lost, perhaps magnolia shadows
best summarised that passing into transience.
How briefly flowers became pink, fragile shells
in gardens with a long view to the sea.

Leaves shielded heat, and patterned overlaps,
changing all shades of green, all flickering shadows
that gave space, like field or outdoor room
angled to opened sky like attic skylight.

Not practical to stay when growing older,
bus stop eight miles away, rough track to road.
We left it with the jacket weaved from upland,
all colours of the fell above the cottage.

Not really garden, more a patch of ground
laid out by others with more knowledge, patience,
planting magnolia as stranger, out of place,
tenant among oaks, yet growing to that woodland.

Safe Home

House hunting; out for somewhere to call home,
brought a return to a half-remembered hamlet
on a winter's afternoon, air stung by coal smoke,
a shunt of railway cottages like a branch line.

Nothing moved, except for a local cyclist.
He warned of the house next door, of noise, and strangers.
A train passed, non-stop through the former station
where once steam showed which way the wind was blowing.

Each village, then, had a halt and station master,
an hourly service each could set his watch by.
Lines still ran parallel to roads and fells
spreading last firebox orange on recent snowfall.

A small road from a junction, like a crossing,
led past the rippled metal of a buckled barn,
past wintering-out tired arable, slashed and scarred
with tweed ruts that last tractor wove on leaving,

reminder of departure. She must have felt
a gathering pulse against her neck, rail tighten
as a late express approached. She lay flat out,
singer without a note, in usual black.

Like her a poet, on a night train going back,
sharing his flask, a dram, a line; chance meeting;
and when we left his reading voice rang out:
Thank you for listening! Travel well! Safe home!

Early Closing

Each day is early closing this midwinter,
moon up and about by five as constellations
of lamps define the towns across the landscape.

Shopping is what we find in stoop and gather,
snapped ash for kindling strewn by gale-force weather.

In cities stores scent entrances to acres,
assistants groomed in place, while background music
sets tune and tone for buying dream and magic,

as escalators offer angel flightpaths,
ascending and descending like the lost myths.

Perhaps this is the ladder from earth to heaven
where there is no night, just the scans' surveillance?

While in the other world where wild is witness
a fox may scorch the verge with moonlight, ashen,
and kestrels, furling wings, sense the west darken.

Solstice

Plaid landscape, blotted with lichen; bronze-aged moorland.
Standing stones tell the time in angled sunlight,
sundial, or burial ground; rehearsed cathedral.

Strangers track information boards, and yet
no-one knows chapter and verse for this wild siting;
stockade of rock and air the pilgrims enter.

All afternoon they pitched up at the encampment,
people who had followed sea-roads to the islands,
slipping through time's boundaries to read the standing stones.

Wind cracked among their hunchbacked tortoise shelters,
and fanned sweet peats to glow the scent of hearths.
Some toured the waiting megaliths' ring and aisle

fingering the splintered gneiss. Others shared stories:
I remember only once a solstice sunrise,
silence; then someone asked if they could ring

their Tibetan bell. It must have carried miles,
millennia over moorland. Everyone
turned to shake hands, with chimes still echoing.

Most would stay up all night, wait out the dark
till dawn at four, like people of any century
exchanging tales, passing some singing round.

We left before nightfall, returning to our present century,
hearing at all hours in the attic room
Atlantic storm on skylights, seeking entrance,

morse on the glass, as tapping into the past,
that stone plan of the Celtic cross as forecast
three thousand years before it was enacted.

Lent

Driving to Lent

Driving to Lent under the cover of darkness
there is barely a car on the back road following the river,
but creatures are out: oil slick of a water rat,
rear light white scut of a roe deer near the wood,
black and white weight of a badger rambling to arable,
and owl that veers through our lights
    with its landing flaps lowered.
They know we have forty days of desert, and listening.
They attend, and will wait on night,
    through the late Spring's coming.

Lent

Lent brings to Spring at least a double meaning;
drought-time of searching in some wilderness,
also remortgage for each loan of years,
reminder we are stewards of this yearning season.
Paradox: that back roads towards the desert
are lined with pioneer blossom, unfolding hawthorn;
that forty days below slate quarry cloud banks
bear miners' lamps of gorse towards thorn's crowning.

North

Going North I would always take the bird book,
gift become ritual, knowing the oystercatchers
marking the cover would be waiting on
facing the wind along a slab of shoreline.
An outdoor gospel, its plastic cover rippled
from rubbing in jacket pockets, watermarked
during that island downpour when the thunder
washed out the evidence of any species.

The Rock Dove

Never at home with pigeons, he found the dove
inadequate symbol over baptismal waters;
weak manifesto for a revolutionary.
That occasion called out for an untamed herald.
Enter a theologian with an eye for birds
who re-translated the text into a rock dove,
nesting, at home at the far end of a cave
deep in the dark, at edge of God, and nightfall.

Spirit Level

Someone has opened their hands; a flock of music
lifts over pews, and carved stalls in the abbey choir
as a curlew, not missing a beat, would glide
to follow a single note with an anthem of moorland.
We are stopped in our tracks, and pools form in prints
    round our footsteps;
hear the range of an echo, as wind comes over the edge
of west horizons, ruled steady as a spirit level.
We are called, like the man in the boat, to walk on the water.

Prayer

Now any prayer must be offered in the open,
at one with chant of burn, below the whispered
breeze in the oaks above the burial ground,
twenty miles from a kirk these days of absence.
Distance is also quiet; a scrap of gull
cries out in white against a soaked, slate sky.
Prayer is the venture capital of listening.
Answer is parable, that keeps its distance.

Correspondences

Football and politics are off the agenda,
and when I drop a line you rarely answer.
You don't believe in god or climate change
but like to visit churches, watch The Weather.
Perhaps, like prayer, some silence is correspondence?
Sometimes, in church, with more cold weather forecast,
I sympathise, and offer words to silence,
and wonder if, given time, there'll be an answer.

TV Times

They must meet behind closed doors, and share diversions,
draft dreams for screen, devising spells and visions,
some other world's alternative reality.
Given the famines, given the mounds of clothes
that are those sleepers curled up under stairwells,
there's need for lights and yells, given the wars,
need tunes that audiences could tap their feet to;
given the encroaching storm, sequins and dancers.

Reflection

Given a morning when chilled air is stilled,
and everything is doubled: the attendant trees
obedient to the profile of the fells,
ridges that forge an arrow in anchored water
as wedge or wake, as signpost pointing inland;
one careless stone could shatter whole reflected sky
brimming where lake has drowned near vertical screes,
as one cruel word could rupture peace that's lodged there.

Scree

Presence: a million tons of rock are coned
into the scree that slants a thousand feet
from spread of lake to ridge, a growling poise
guttural with threat of drop as avalanche.
Passage is a narrow way across, the path
buckled and lost into odd boulder tumble.
Walkers must pick their way; wilderness mobile.
The risk of further fall is always present.

The Ghost Door

Now that the coat of arms is taken down
and the church wall's free to breathe from domination,
and plaster's sloughed clean like a healed leper's skin,
the old west door's disclosed, like one from a tomb,
finding his way with unbound eyes, yet questioning.
Rough lintel at head height needs reverencing
through infilled entrance like rough lines of prayer
breathing again, as though a seal was broken.

Shutters

Came with the cottage, hinged doors over windows
dated as mid-Victorian. You imagine
those panels folded over as light was leaving,
pulled from recess to frame the verticals,
becoming proxy windows every evening.
Third month of wearied year, again we turn
calendar pages to reach those opening views;
to counteract the glass gaps in the shutters,
slashed Lenten light; this other side of nightfall.

Lancet Windows

Saints must be slim to sentry lancet windows,
holding their breaths for centuries, framed in stone,
adopting biblical paths, the narrow ways,
trim as the angels' ladder, veins of vine.
Victorians took them over, upstairs rooms
in cottages given eye-level, vertical glass
archers or holy people would have welcomed;
Lent's indoor dusk, as under gathering skies.

Lights

North sky was weaving greens, the Northern Lights
had come south bridging counties on the Solway,
draping the night with mossed plaid, staining limestone
and crippled winter yews, and sandstone gravestones.
A friend told of one eve of Lent, on Orkney,
among stone sentinels at the Ring of Brodgar,
when suddenly the Lights came out to make it timeless,
and set the women, and the shadows, dancing.

Gift

Where would it last be worn to hang its future,
that friendship gift from one no longer travelling
out to the islands? What might it once have held
in pockets scarred by thorn, with an inch of tear?
It carries an expensive name on roundels where
they are clipped on flaps over odd pocket baggage:
notebook to note birds winging on freshening weather,
some fingerless mittens to warm hands for pen-holding.

Present

An aerial view from the top of a double-decker
shows streets of shops, long corridors of commerce
in what appears to be a capital's custom
of outdoor stalls of fruit in plastic baskets:
small globes of oranges, apples, peaches, limes.
A customer's served, and as he counts small coinage
the seller laughs, and drops a large banana
into his shopping bag, free, and shakes his hand.

South

We woke up over Kinshasa; aerial screens
showing a nudge south-east towards Johannesburg.
All night we had tracked down Africa in a hiss
of air, as following swifts above the Sahara.
'How did you come?' the grounded congregation
asked in a bush stick-church, a fortnight later.
Miracle to them. They climbed back on a lorry
for grit and sand tracks home; all the way singing.

West to East

Sandstone instead of granite laid foundations;
wide skies are raftered with fine strips of cloud
rather than lapped slate slanting the layered fells.
Fields angle south for grain and sunlight harvest
west-east, share lanes where turn of tarmac dwindles
into foundation gravel, where hedges rise,
become horizons of blackthorn, hawthorn, ash,
pacing the odd half-mile in each direction.

Warning

Red thumbprint in the east as though the sky
at five this time of year is manuscript,
and someone caught the edge with sealing wax
before the scroll's rolled, or the seal has set.
Otherwise leaded light in shades of grey:
imagine a shepherd scanning the spine of dale
reading a warning from the children's rhyme
of weather like a wolf pack over the fell.

Indoor Weather

That poise within the evening when fresh water
speckles the skylight, and we read the rain
as something alien, best kept out of doors,
wolves in the wind, wild, something we fear.
Strange that we write of it behind closed windows,
that hiss of downpour dumbed by double glazing,
as prophecy hidden within the gift of tongues
is muted by a hesitant translation.

Painting Weather

John, you paint weather, taking us along
that track towards The Cheviot as green wind
rifles new leaves in a dress rehearsal of Spring.
You have marshalled browns, from fawns to mahogany,
as a wintering chapter of page-rustling beech,
catching each leaf as steeped in sunlight, shadow.
It is calm in your room, where Christ, out of the evening,
is offering a grace in memory of Caravaggio.

Revisiting Rembrandt

First Lent sky, with a west wind blading the mills
in his imagination, revisiting Rembrandt
by turning pages on polders and canals,
and meeting those self-portraits eye to eye.
He felt that man would also know his sadness,
despite the celebration of freshening weather
the other side of glass, as if the world
he conjured, sought fresh air, and liberation.

Air

One friend arrives by train, checks in for a dawn
call for a flight to Amsterdam, then Nairobi.
Four hours by train would take him through a zebra
landscape, home, to where he'll plant a farm.
Two others might have crossed his path at thirty thousand
feet as they tracked west, Kolkata into Glasgow.
Meanwhile, for all those miles we take our dog
across the fields, below an occasional flightpath.

Collie

Watch, and you'll find his shadow padding stillness
in black and white against the camouflage
of moss and sedge, treacle brown of sagged peat.
Call, and he'll turn aside again to greet you.
You might explain to him that you've moved on,
that each return is just a cast of memory,
mobile as sunlight, aerial as scale of larks.
Leave, and he'll slip away down the ache of nightfall.

Search

Hardly a soul about. We left our collie
shivering from echoed shots across the valley.
Odd squall. A Lenten dusk; a sense of waiting;
yet even after death a continuing search
combing eternity for one called 'lost',
that friend's dead brother, the subject of her prayer:
He will not look for you; please look for him.
One light beyond bare trees begins to move.

Temple

A military congregation; Roman faithful
coming in out of the wind besieging moorland
to peaceful flicker of lamps. They faced across
an aisle as if rehearsing college chapel.
Barely ten soldiers' strides from door to altar,
now just a plan, no higher than a shin guard.
A passing walker leaves a sweet as offering;
curlews continue centuries of veneration.

Child

He was born as hostage under military occupation,
roads clogged with census refugees, the homeless
desperate for even a foxhole to lay their heads.
(A bed was beyond their means from war's inflation.)
Child's cry in stables showed the homeless crisis,
farm labourer shortage meant some shepherds stayed
out on the hill, while later comrades told
about a carpenter's lad; some straw, a manger.

Sleepers

They lie, bundled in winter, sleeping-bagged, under
a stairwell. One turns over as shoppers pass.
It is mid-morning. All that they have, their gifts,
are bagged up as a bit of insulation.
They should be up and about on a begging shift.
They are nameless; only three, perhaps returning
from somewhere lit by a star, or stranded where
they sought a new way home, as dreams demanded.

Waving at Trains

He had gone to stretch his legs at a hundred miles
an hour on the express train non-stop between
Durham and Kings Cross, across the English steppes,
flat land defining nowhere in particular,
speed ripping off the names of minor stations.
Then, slowing for some reason, long enough
to see someone, a boy, with nothing to do
but wave at trains, as welcome and farewell.

The Film-maker

(in memory of Derek Jarman)

Durham, York, Doncaster, Stevenage,
the non-stop stations rule the rails to London;
and even further south, where ground meets water,
poet, film director, gardener; victim of AIDS.
I find his grave, and read of flowers he found
on Channel shingle, and weave a wreath for him:
larkspur, wild pansy, snapdragon, sow thistle, vetch;
hare's foot, herb Robert, sun sperge, evening primrose.

Legacies

What do they leave when they become the strangers?
Sometimes a house, or even a wealth of acres,
a library, redundant pictures, silverware;
more often a rack of clothes, outdated armchairs;
or just, if they have been moved into a home,
parts of their past to fit that single room:
those few left-overs after the rest was sent
with their stick to the charity shop, just before closing.

Recycling

Lids were screwed to the underside of shelving
so that the contents of each jar were clear.
Pride of place went to the six inch nails,
and steel bolts that could hold strong beams together.
Barbed wire was coiled in a corner for a murderer's plaiting,
and beams were stacked in racks according to span
needed to hammer blows to outstretched arms,
and jars of leather threads for wrists and ankles.

Follower

Thirty years passed. He felt he should return
to see who the child had become, yet everywhere
he was told the travelling teacher had moved on.
Some recalled stories, others a healing gift.
Some felt he would go to the city for the holy feast.
And afterwards, despite the miraculous stories,
the road led on again to places of pain,
some telling of wounded hands; a hawthorn crown.

After

Some take to the roads again, after the pause,
to hear the old story sung by candlelight,
eat festive food, together find the stars
clear on a sharp night, given a new companion;
look back to wonder what new months might bring,
that new moon of a strand with oystercatchers.
Some tenancy at frayed edges of used maps;
staff and boots at the doorway for departure.

Poorly

The child had never been to church before,
but found between ice creams, Italian shadows,
a 'poorly man' on sticks, hanging about.
He wondered who he was, and how to help him.
Lots to explain: long ago, place and time,
how he shared gifts of making people better,
telling them stories that would change their lives.
I've never heard of him. Where to begin?

Broken

Far, far worse than the record; a decent flogging
would leave the body open like a slaughtered bullock
before the blood was hosed; a hawthorn crown
would skewer pain deep, into the brow, and mind,
each wince another wound as insults lanced him.
And the women watched from far as crosses rocked
in piercing lightning, screaming with imploring arms
held impotently against the deaths, and deluge.

Grief (Gaza)

Women have grieved again in recent times
among the tombs of ruins where their families lie,
stones rolled by air strikes. Crabbed hands claw clear sky
that moulds a dome above the drift of shrouds.
Now many a son is missing, and distraught friends
can only absorb rank grief like a vinegared sponge.
They bulldoze a garden grave to reach the dead.
We watch as we jingle thirty pieces of silver.

Answering the Shoah

An old wound; open, weeping, festering, raw,
a trial by fire without redemptive verdict;
stain spread so deep no blood can seem to cleanse it:
total six million, each beyond calculation,
so other violence, part of dead reckoning.
Although one Jew, arms racked to global wingspan,
still comes from time to time, from past to future
as sacrifice; as offering an answer.

Woodwork

Sorrow has grained cowled faces in the monks' oak sculpture.
They are bearing on tired shoulders their abbot's coffin,
one step ahead of strangers who would ransack
chapel, scriptorium for the hell of it.
Intent in Lent they are seeking a resting place,
their habits adzed to the anxious pace of searching.
They sense fresh breeze of his departed breath,
that stirs the patient wood they have been carved from.

Gold

Driving back, just the two of them on the fell road,
not so much tarmac as a cloth of gold
laid out to turn the sky to an inland ocean
of slowly rising, falling swell of upland.
Long evening waters; his life then on the ebb,
so all the more valued that dividend of the sea
he had relished from the cottage, a reaching light
that seemed to stay till ways home were accomplished.

Lament

Walking Distance

(Southport: July 2024)

Christ was there first in flickering black and white,
his ministry interrupted while they changed
reels on the Bell and Howell church hall projector.

We never saw his face. It was not that sort
of time and place for intimate revelations.
Later the sound of old hymns died away

all over the town. Such chapels turned into mosques.
Fewer came for the sea air, and the flowers.
Yet little girls danced for joy to Taylor Swift

until the murderer with a knife came round,
and young and brave joined headlines, bulletins,
official statistics, casualty lists, memorials.

That summer's evening, wreathed with scent of flowers,
thousands bowed at the vigil. Others came,
brought hate without a shred of evidence,

murdering the quiet, and the quiet respect,
torching a police van for the hell of it,
stoning the police who tried to guard the mosque.

All this short walking distance from once home.
Christ of the stabbed side, and nailed-healing hands
might reach through blood and ash; know each by name.

Tracing Rembrandt

Suddenly as we pass through various galleries,
passing the weight of gilt that frames the angels,
they give way to wind-driven Dutch galleon cloud banks
pouring inland to shadow Rembrandt's studio.

Studious, he is all eyes, watching for the slightest movement
in the portrait waiting for that touch, to finish.
Nobody knows who Paul the saint resembled
but Rembrandt knew. He shared that recognition;

that older man he chanced on in a side-street,
or among the watchfulness of a fellow artist.
Perhaps he invited him home, asked him to sit,
sketched his years quickly, as the light was fading.

Only his face is fully lit, and his hands
clasped in the shape of a heart that might be breaking.
His gaze is deepening with dark as though some news
has stilled his eyes, hooding them with apprehension.

We do not see his clothes, but know they match
an old coat we might choose to enter autumn.
An Elderly Man as St Paul in the seventeenth century
becomes the face an evening mirror catches.

A matt black frame contains him, yet his vision
is stretched as a parchment reaching for the eternal.

A man made blind by light, brought home by exile;
a silenced scholar rich with the gift of tongues.

We draw close; just a brush's grip away,
translating Rembrandt's gaze, his palette of shadows
as he might check low light that ripples a forehead;
as he might stand, before a completing gesture.

Self-Portrait with Maulstick, Palette and Brushes

The book is left open to show a late self-portrait.
Rembrandt, alone, has cast himself as witness.
Wherever an observer moves his gaze will follow.

He watched himself at work, a mirror fixed
to his easel at an angle of reflection;
pictured himself, whatever he was painting:

landscape or seascape, windmill, or a prodigal son,
beggar on a doorstep, militia setting out;
space that disclosed a miracle, or a crucifixion.

All reproductions struggle to catch his palette,
greyish green underpainting, comments a critic;
pinks, oranges, yellows set his features up.

Tools gained their status by title; brushes staked
as out of focus flowers; the maulstick, rested
as one straight line among the question-marks.

New worlds are waiting like the untenanted globes
outlined on the studio wall in the frantic quiet;
his restless gaze on fire with concentration.

Pictures

Three greyhounds: they have heard something beyond
moor's customary vocabulary, on the long wind
that carries the curlew's anguish, sheep's fracturing
bleating; the insistent hissing of cotton grass.

Suddenly they are alert, rigid in the electric,
their faces sharpened by that shaft of sound.
Gold frame in which they are held inside the gallery
pens them, but the land beyond is ocean.

Next painting is abstract geometry, perhaps a town
grey, green, brown angles, river's silver waver.
Untenanted, lacking even the shepherd, or drover
who come down out of the wind from moorland passage.

We pause before a landscape, in a lay-by;
become that place a moment, sense that space
an artist caught and tamed in glass, and frame.
We stretch arms wide when no-one else is watching.

Ammonite

He turned flat circle of stone over and over,
feeling against his thumb sharp print of furrows
like fresh plough hardening under a blade of frost,
spiral of ridges coiled to a mudstone vortex.

Shell become stone, mollusc turned ammonite,
fossil of sea creature; once both rudder and sail.
Held, it became a comma, or a question-mark
to Genesis dating. Days became millions of years.

Laid across text it makes a paperweight
against the numbered verses and annotations
of the black book shivering in chilled candlelight
as draught seeps under a door, as a storm gathers.

Flame shines brass spine and snuffer, gold emerging
like dawn within first morning of creation.
He took a pen to set the record straight,
knew nothing was set in stone, but negotiation.

Antler

Almost a plant in resemblance to root and branch,
stem rounded off to a stump of amputation,
cream and brown, the veins of a bone's song,
found without reference to stag in island bracken.

He handled it again, a final time,
weighing its balance like a bow across his fingers.
No trophy, and lacking reference, incomplete;
once taken out on loan; and now returning.

The island could provide a mourning ground
facing the west, toward the end of days,
like a traveller coming into sanctuary space;
slight drag in his shoulder bag, medieval pace.

Wait: to read the chapel before entering,
its roof long gone, one gable fretted by weather,
the other thatched with late summer's seeded grass;
few lights from dandelions' occasional crowns,

and odd thorns prickling sky like a tiara.
And in the bending low, and holding still
the view was a slice of Sound through doorless arches,
the psalm a sigh of tide, and gulls' responses.

He paused before placing the horn with its sickle curves
to raise an asbestos lid shielding a gravestone
showing stags rearing in fear from a hunting horn;
a carved woman waiting for news, cradling an otter.

Almost a reverence as he laid his gift
in a niche beside the altar space. It went,
taken in the couple of days before he checked:
only an echo of bellow in a rising wind,
only the stain of a stag left in a shadow.

Ruin

This ruin is knee-high, end on to the water,
croft house reduced to its plan, its boulders taken
to hem some grazing, settle a boundary cairn.

Once it would chime with voices; talk of tides,
the flow of fishing weather; news that the deer
had moved off over the hill as a storm warning.

Once a woman, whose clan had learned this landscape,
might have spread wide with her weaving a Gaelic psalm
that summoned the otters, and the silver shoal,

might have caught the oystercatchers' alarm,
piercing and piping, of how that land might change,
and praise become lament; welcome, departure,

presence become absence. Soon the nets were furled,
the hired cart lashed down for the plodding away
as late light paved the road, as the stranger came.

Clearances

1.

That second sunset warned them: factor's men
had come with flints and locks, made families vagrant,
had fired their thatch while fathers fought the French.
A low wind bore lament in cindering weather.

2.

Skeletons are still there; land an obituary
for tumbled bones of cottages, sightless windows
that once glanced to the grazing for the fathers,
but saw just Englished shadows as the light fled.

After, the wrenched off doors became the eaves
leaned against rain as legacy of shelter.
Spilt milk hissed out the hearths after the looms
were laid across ashed peats to cease the weaving.

Sometimes a length of plaid was cut to rescue,
binding them on the uncertain trek to exile.

3.

Today, in another country, clans might lose
their place where time has nurtured their olive trees
felled out of conquest, as grubbing history out,
forced with their flocks from centuries of grazing.

A shepherd's last glance might note the conqueror's star
blue as a cleared sky, lacking compassionate shelter.
Bulldozers come to gnaw familiar walls.
Rifles might crack, and other settlers follow.

What had they learned? Indictment of their people's pain
read over as dark harvest spreads again.

4.

Spring brimmed the Auschwitz ash pits, livening spawn.
Few watch towers sentry, miles of wire constrain.
It was not that long ago, in biblical time.
Now West Bank adds new fractions to the six million.

Loch

Loch remained rumour, blue blot on the map
till that final moment. After the tarmac start
we rubbled gravel, passing a picket of pines
to deer-grazed turf, after the track ran out.

And never just about water, also skies
it held in passing, unfurling and overlapped.
In summer still enough of an overflow
to clear the throat of stonework down a channel,

half-ruin of long foundation, rippling on
under the sagging handrail of a gap-flagged bridge,
rusted industrial plaque now written off;
clotted reeds flattened black in iris twilight.

Never just about water, but infilled air
flowing with whimbrels like rehearsing curlew.
We went to see them again, when we went back,
but found they had flown, and left only a rumour.

Trod

Each autumn they sailed eastwards to the mainland,
revisiting that harbour of dale and fells,
and walked the contour lines along the hills.

They learned terms as the colours thinned and deepened,
how track was called a trod, and ewes were yows,
how hill became a pike in dialect voice,

learned knack to loose the sneck that clasped the gate,
as lilt of lift, so hooked hasp on the chain
came up as echoed note, and five bars opened

to passage, well-prepared; a concave walk
veined in a slope driven deep by cart and tractor,
once hobnail trudge of miners' leaded labour

sentried by oaks. Centuries since someone's vision
tamped saplings home to vary hazel woodland
where winter finds its way with catkin lanterns.

Time, then, to plot a route for later height
where trees give way along the edge of sky
as seeing the lake framed through a needle's eye.

They named the track, or trod, after their island,
remembering also slight wear on the machair
through scents blown off Atlantic, gorse flares, clover.

Evening will fill the arch of trees, allow
gleaning of kindling from the most recent storm;
aerials of oak and beech west wind snapped down.

Pause, as a blackbird wards off camouflaged dark
stillness is shivered by a stung hail shower.
They wait, to count the silver on the water.

Gap

After the storm a craftsman brought his name,
Makepeace, to redeem the desolation,
taking away felled trees to catch their grain
in new forms, like the welcome of an armchair.

His skill and insight, turning and imagination
needed again where the sycamore was felled
that plugged the Gap along the Roman Wall
sprouting two centuries out of the roll of hills,

alert like the quiver of aerials when gale stripped out
its shadow to skeleton in long winter seasons,
as listening out for stories; the tramp of legions,
crows' warning; liquid ripple of a gliding curlew.

Chain sawed down in a night in a land dispute
said one obituary. Hope that its stump might sprout.
Its timber was carted off as a trailer load,
ground where it stood blank signpost to the angered North,

rumour of saga that each strong wind will carry.
Given a season in a drying shelter
it could yield harvest, chair, table, a ring of bowls,
a gathering of peace and place as response to violence.

Sapling

Once they were on the roads they found so many
bowed in their black coats, scrolls of sentences
stitched into linings, silenced; watching their steps.

Leaving the streets as exiles from ruined cities
they made their way to where the desert waited,
feeling the evenings darkening, drained of hope.

Thousands. They could have overcome the guards
but no-one made a gesture of resistance,
except the woman who bent to pluck a chestnut

out of the verge, and stow it in her double lining.
She dared to speak one midnight as fitful fires
turned to ash, and many succumbed to nightmares.

She whispered that she planned return, survival,
bringing the sapling nurtured from her planting
to add it to a copse, with oak and rowan.

No-one

No-one lives in Wales. Turn calendar pages
from spring to summer, Ebrill into Gorffennaf,
and the pictures show water, and stone, but nobody present.

Right from the start, translated into January,
high in the mountains, under a shroud of snow,
there seems to be no presence, hand or footprint.

Even by waters, blurred in the photograph,
by a slowness of camera setting, shot from the knees
like a penitent, praying, the grass remains unmarked.

Such absence informed the poems of RS Thomas,
a writing priest, who set out seeking God
in empty churches, on blank sheets of paper,

waiting, unprinted like frozen folds of snow,
tracking the emptiness of water and stone
until the weather brought a resolve of thaw.

He wrote then how he set his telescope
focused on emptiness, and watched the sea
for evidence of presence, gathered wings.

Scholar of God's truancy he'd turn for home,
stand in his angled churchyard, pray the names
of others stilled to stone, carved landward facing

shallow fields tilled to gruel, thin-shepherded.
Perhaps he'd watch the island's whale back profile
till dusk brought fade, to take that day away,

number and name, like autumn in both his tongues,
translating absence into presence again.
He might stay in case of an echo in the evening.

RS Thomas on Bardsey

He patrolled boundaries, between his Welsh and English,
speaking both tongues almost in opposition
like shepherds struggling their livings off the hills.

Priest, he was pastor to the words around him,
working west through some parishes till the evening
outlined the island on a wealth of silver.

He'd take note: slate walls host to chimes of thrift,
ruled fields set square, the candlestick of lighthouse,
few trees; that hunchback thorn with a crown's profile.

At home with flight he watched the birds' migrations
passing at an angle to the prevailing wind
like questions during a sermon. He would set

his glass on open water's swirl of danger,
and watch in case a stranger, like a prophet,
came out of nowhere; settled into focus.

Some said he walked too close to Bible namesake,
absent and doubtful on that Easter evening,
needing to touch nail scars, that fresh-scabbed side,

knowing the loneliness of absence, darkness
that falls as black as cassock on that island:
shearwaters coming ashore, into its sanctuary.

Bird Book

Frayed on the leading edge as if wings caught
flap of wax jacket pocket on some moorland,
as flock breaks skyline, needing identity.

Pages thumbed concave; peat stain as postmark
like airmail sent first-class by owl or whimbrel;
a watermark from thunder in the open.

Those odd notes on a watching in the margins;
places, and dates, low flight of weather sharpening
focus on profile, plumage, spread of wings.

Gift from a friend, no longer fit to follow
her own tug of migration to the islands;
remembering that shared morning, watching choughs,

curlews' arrival, bringing evening inland.
She borrowed the book back, in her suburban close;
heard that held note, still, unfurling over horizons.

Reunion

Just six or seven went on to The Bull
with smiled excuse of *What she would have wanted.*
White wine at four: *Oh, I'll just have a large one.*

Old friends rejoined from varied geography,
Cumbria to Bucks., and also round the corner,
each given as birthday cards her water-colours,

that curlew pacing out an evening tideline,
choughs' shadows against a cliff face, swallows' skirl;
close-ups of wing and bill; the wild brought closer.

Another before we go? Thoughts turned to miles
into the evening: drive to that other side
of her adopted city, or change of trains,

the unspoken: how the visitors had winced
at preacher's platitudes; how they'd watched her fade
into a shadowed parable of grief.

Reunion, too, went home; left empty glasses
holding half-measures of sunlight. No one said:
Until we meet again, about the next one.

Personal

Most news is second handing-on, but sorrow
is personal as a name. That death of a friend
coming into her phone on a walk in mid-winter,

a shell's message, brief, just fitting the palm of her hand,
stilling the day like the sudden shelter of beech copse,
the turn of the valley misting, and suddenly cold.

Pause to remember the hours where the width of her smile
stretched out the world like sunlight patching a landscape.
She remembered those times through the drift of the late
evening news:

war again, distant yet close as the sitting-room screen,
drumming of rain on the plastic of refugees' shelter;
the distant and far coming close at the press of a button.

Each day she would take to the copse at the end of the silence
a small stone as letter to spell out the cost of her absence.

Wreaths

He mourned them all, as if the gospel writers
had died of AIDS, with David, Terry, Howard:
Goodnight Johnny, goodnight boys
who lay in the bed that I lie on.

And walking over the shingle at Dungeness,
as if the funerals had just been honoured,
he listed all the evening still in flower
and wrote a wreath of words for each of them:

opium poppy, scabious, sea pink, alkanet,
white clover, rest harrow, wild carrot, woody nightshade,
mustard, mayweed, camomile, mallow, daisy,
larkspur, snapdragon, sow thistle, tufted vetch,
hare's foot, herb Robert, sun sperge, evening primrose.

The Haunting

Today he is just a photograph, a boy
dressed in his best; dark jacket, and crew-neck gansey
over his white shirt, fashionable check flared trousers;
his anorak stowed behind him, like a life-raft.

He is all at sea, not looking at the water,
but back, inland, eyes cast down in the small
sort of fishing boat his father rented,
working North Sea for plaice, a box of lobsters,

lost, really, on such known, familiar waters,
taken out, first trip since his father downed.
Someone well-meaning must have planned the voyage.

Today he is just a caption, one among
the many mourners after a boat was tipped.
He does not read the sky; his gaze is dipped.

Staff

I offered him the staff, but he declined it.
I rather saw its future on his island,
a passing-on, new chapter in its history
that started with the friend who made it for me.

He'd checked the road was empty before he climbed
the chained gate with its sign forbidding entrance,
melding his bow-saw close to match his profile,

quickly at work to trim a length of hazel
height of a stride to steady on rough pasture.
Laid-down, a drying-out of seasons' moisture.

Then drilling to thread a lanyard, shoeing its foot
with a metal ferrule; then final glaze of varnish.
Perhaps a stroll to test its walking pace,
a handing-over: *While you recuperate.*

It needed a change of place, as levering
the mountain like a punt pole taking flood
through rock and sedge, as steadying the stance,
emerging to sky's light; the world spread out
to all the islands scattered on the ocean.

Pity that it never went. If I return
perhaps I'll take it to an island cottage
where silence stays, and seals map out the inlet,
and leave it in a porch, beside a boot-rack.

Walking Home

(in memory of Mick McFadyen)

If light stays we'll retrace his favourite walk,
leaving the church, to rise along the lonnen
where grass is coming back through crumbling tarmac,

and gaining height brings, after copse and outcrop,
a majesty of firth, the other country
that put Mc into his name, and grounded him.

Each footstep as memorial; what he valued,
remembering how the west wind turned an ash
into a sculpture of a peacock's skeleton,

how clints and grikes made pavement over pasture,
how Northern Lights turned cloud to unripe harvest,
and how the evening curlews tuned concertos.

We crossed two counties returning to his resting,
parish we'd shared, that first green hill in England;
the trig point where the world regained perspective.

He stayed on in the slim ground loaned to him.
His parable walking home, under a rainbow.

Requiem

(in memory of John Burnside)

Dusk; when we realise we have never owned
this day, but rather it was something lent.
Trees meet to weave his name, tonight as requiem,

and wait; as he might stand inside a wood
in border light, and stay for night to come,
summoning wild creatures always dear to him.

He sent out words to question faith at twilight,
those echoes from black scriptures, and the Mass;
that tentative pace towards the sign of the cross.

And if we'd met, what more for us to say
than what he had written already, enlightening days,
boyhood's creeds always with him, like a shade,

lightening our darkness, opening those possible years;
calling us from the far side of the trees?

Notes

The Greatcoat takes reference from the novel of the same name by Helen Dunmore.

Single dates from 1967 when I spent a month in former Czechoslovakia on a student exchange. On our return journey a young woman hid in our compartment to cross into 'The West'. Had we been in Prague exactly a year later, we would have been caught up in the Russian invasion.

The Japanese Department moves between theory and reality; between visiting a university department of Japanese studies, and Japan itself. Here, in a modern hotel, one room was a replica of a traditional farmhouse as representing a negotiation between the country's past and present.

Whaup is the Scottish term for a curlew.

Safe Home brings together three memories linked by railways: a search for a new home in the North of England, the suicide of a friend some years before, and meeting a poet on a train. His farewell, 'Safe home!', proved both moving and ironic.

Ammonite imagines an early English geologist sensing the coming theological turmoil as the study of fossils challenged the then traditional dating of the age of the world based on supposed biblical calculations.

Gap concerns the felling of the tree – made globally famous in a sequence in the film *Robin Hood Prince of Thieves* – at Sycamore Gap on Hadrian's Wall in September 2023. Two men from Cumbria were charged with criminal damage, which they denied.

Wreaths takes reference from *Pharmacopoeia: A Dungeness Notebook* (Vintage Classics 2022) by the film-maker, poet, artist and botanist Derek Jarman in which he laments the deaths of friends who died from AIDS but also celebrates the plants he found on an evening walk near his cottage on the shingle bank at Dungeness, in Kent. *The Film-maker* offers a similar tribute.

The poem also takes reference from Michael Longley's elegy on the Irish 'Troubles', *The Ice-Cream Man*.

About the author

Martyn Halsall grew up in Southport, then in Lancashire, taught in Dorset, and was a student in Chelsea, London before becoming a journalist. After reporting for local and regional newspapers he joined *The Guardian* as a staff correspondent; later working as a communications advisor in the Church of England. He has published six poetry pamphlets, and *Lent* is his fourth full collection. He is married to Isobel, an Anglican priest, and lives and writes in Northumberland.